IELTS Reading Practice Tests:

IELTS Guide for Self-Study Test Preparation for IELTS for Academic Purposes

IELTS is jointly owned by the British Council, IDP: IELTS Australia, and Cambridge English Language Assessments, which are neither affiliated with nor endorse this publication.

IELTS Reading Practice Tests: IELTS Guide for Self-Study Test Preparation for IELTS for Academic Purposes

© COPYRIGHT 2014 IELTS Success Associates

All rights reserved. No part of this publication may be reproduced, stored in a retrieval system, or transmitted, in any form or by any means, electronic, mechanical, photocopying, recording, or otherwise, without the prior written permission of the copyright owner.

ISBN-13: 978-1-949282-23-8
ISBN-10: 1-949282-23-6

NOTE: IELTS is jointly owned by the British Council, IDP: IELTS Australia, and Cambridge English Language Assessments, which are neither affiliated with nor endorse this publication.

TABLE OF CONTENTS

IELTS Reading Exam Information	1
Instructions to Candidates – IELTS Reading	3
IELTS Reading Exam Format	5
IELTS Reading Exam Question Types	6
How to Use This Publication	8
IELTS Practice Reading – Test 1 Answer Sheet	9
IELTS Practice Reading – Test 1:	
TEST 1 – READING PASSAGE 1	10
TEST 1 – READING PASSAGE 2	18
TEST 1 – READING PASSAGE 3	25
Reading Test 1 – Answer Key	31
Reading Test 1 – Explanations to the Answers	33
IELTS Practice Reading – Test 2 Answer Sheet	47
IELTS Practice Reading – Test 2:	
TEST 2 – READING PASSAGE 1	48
TEST 2 – READING PASSAGE 2	54
TEST 2 – READING PASSAGE 3	61
Reading Test 2 – Answer Key	66
Reading Test 2 – Explanations to the Answers	69

IELTS Practice Reading – Test 3 Answer Sheet	80
IELTS Practice Reading – Test 3:	
TEST 3 – READING PASSAGE 1	81
TEST 3 – READING PASSAGE 2	87
TEST 3 – READING PASSAGE 3	92
Reading Test 3 – Answer Key	97
Reading Test 3 – Explanations to the Answers	99

IELTS Reading Exam Information

The reading part of the IELTS test is similar for the Academic Purposes and General Training Modules.

The Academic Module will contain passages that are factual, informative or academic.

The General Training Module will contain the same types of passages as the Academic Module.

In addition, you may see instructions, advertisements, or information bulletins on the General Training Module

This publication is written for the IELTS for Academic Purposes Exam, although it can also be used for the IELTS General Training Exam.

The IELTS reading test has three parts. There are 40 questions in total on the reading test and each question is worth one point.

The IELTS reading test lasts for one hour.

As you complete the practice reading tests in this book, you should go quickly from one section to the next in order to make your testing practice as realistic as possible.

Read the instructions for each section of the test and be sure that you answer all of the questions.

When you have completed each practice reading test, check your answers and study the explanations provided.

The instructions for the reading test appear on the next page.

Instructions to Candidates – IELTS Reading

On the real IELTS test, you will see instructions like the following:

- Do not open the test booklet until you are instructed to begin the exam.

- Write your candidate number and name at the top of your answer sheet.

- Read the instructions carefully.

- Be sure to answer all the questions.

- While reading, you may make notes on the exam booklet.

- Use a pencil to write your answers on the answer sheet.

- You must complete the answer sheet for the reading test within the one hour provided. You will not be given extra time when the test finishes to do this.

- You will be asked to hand in your question paper and answer sheet when the test finishes.

- Your score will be based only on the answer sheet.

- The examiners do not consider notes or answers that you may have written on the test booklet.

IELTS Reading Exam Format

There are various formats of questions on the IELTS reading test:

1) Form, diagram or summary completion – you will see a form, diagram or summary and will have to fill in the missing information.

2) Identifying information – you will see a passage which has each paragraph labelled with a specific letter. You will be asked which paragraphs contain specific information.

3) Identifying the writer's views – You will be asked if a list of statements reflect the views of the writer. You will respond: true, false, or not given.

4) Matching features – a list of points or items is provided and these must be matched to a list of categories or groups.

5) Matching headings – you will match a heading or title with the letter of each section from the passage. The heading or title needs to express the main idea of each section of the passage.

6) Multiple choice questions – you will need to choose the correct answer from options A, B or C.

7) Gap fill – you will see a sentence with a gap. You must place a word in the gap. A list of words from which to choose an answer will NOT be provided.

IELTS Reading Exam Question Types

Reading questions on the IELTS Academic Exam can be placed into five broad categories:

1) Main idea questions – You will need to understand the main idea of the passage or of a certain paragraph for these types of questions. You may need to choose your answer from multiple choice options or you may need to match headings or titles with certain sections of the passage.

2) Reading for detail questions – For these types of questions, you will need to scan the passage for the information required and then answer the question. Reading for detail questions can be of any of the following formats: multiple choice, short answer, sentence completion, matching, or form or diagram completion.

3) Making inferences – These questions are not as common as main idea or specific detail questions; however, students often consider inference questions to be the most difficult ones. Inference questions will ask you to find out what idea is implied or indirectly expressed in the passage.

4) Summarising – Below the passage, you will see a summary paragraph containing gaps. You will need to place the correct word in each gap from the list of words provided below the summary.

5) Understanding claims and arguments – These questions will be in the format of identifying the writer's views. So, you will be asked if a list of statements reflect the views of the writer. For each statement, you need to respond: true, false, or not given.

How to Use This Publication

The reading practice tests in this publication contain questions of all of the formats and types that you will see on the real test.

As you complete the practice tests in this book, you should pay special attention to the tips at the beginning of each section of practice test 1. Although you will not see tips like this on the actual exam, these tips will help you improve your performance on each subsequent practice test in this publication.

You should study the explanations to the answers to practice test 1 especially carefully.

The tips that you will see in the questions and explanations to reading practice test 1 will help you obtain strategies to improve your performance on the other practice tests in this book.

Of course, these strategies will also help you do your best on the day of your actual test.

IELTS Practice Reading – Test 1
Answer Sheet

1.	21.
2.	22.
3.	23.
4.	24.
5.	25.
6.	26.
7.	27.
8.	28.
9.	29.
10.	30.
11.	31.
12.	32.
13.	33.
14.	34.
15.	35.
16.	36.
17.	37.
18.	38.
19.	39.
20.	40.

IELTS Practice Reading – Test 1

READING PASSAGE 1

*You should spend about 20 minutes on **Questions 1 to 13** which are based on Reading Passage 1 below:*

SECTION A:

The question of the mechanics of motion is complex and one that has a protracted history. Indeed, much has been discovered about gravity, defined as the force that draws objects to the earth, both before and since the British mathematician Sir Isaac Newton mused upon the subject in the 17th century. As early as the third century BC, a Greek philosopher and natural scientist named Aristotle conducted a great deal of scientific investigation into the subject. In fact, most of Aristotle's life was devoted to the study of the objects of natural science, and it is for this work that he is most renowned. The Greek scientist wrote a tome entitled *Metaphysics*, which contains the observations that he made as a result of performing this original research in the natural sciences.

Several centuries later, in the first century AD, Ptolemy, another Greek scientist, was credited with a nascent, yet unformulated theory, that there was a force that moved toward the centre of the earth, thereby holding objects on its surface. Although later ridiculed for his belief that the earth was the centre of the planetary system, Aristotle's compatriot nevertheless did contribute to the development of the theory of gravity.

SECTION B:

However, it was during the period called the Renaissance that gravitational forces were perhaps studied most widely. An astronomer, Galileo Galilei corrected one of Aristotle's erring theories by pointing out that objects of differing weights fall to earth at the same speed. Years later, Descartes, who was known at that time as a dilettante philosopher, but was later dubbed the father of modern mathematics, held that a body in circular motion constantly strives to recede from the centre. This theory added weight to the notion that bodies in motion have their own forces.

SECTION C:

Newton took these studies a step further, and used them to show that the earth's rotation does not fling bodies into the air because the force of gravity, measured by the rate of falling bodies, is greater than the centrifugal force arising from the rotation. In his first mathematical formulation of gravity, published in 1687, Newton posited that the same force that kept the moon from being propelled away from the earth also applied to gravity at the earth's surface. While this finding, termed the Law of Universal Gravitation, is said to have been occasioned by Newton's observation of the fall of an apple from a tree in the orchard at his home, in reality, the idea did not come to the scientist in a flash of inspiration, but was developed slowly over time.

Newton had the prescience to appreciate that his study was of great import for the scientific community and for society as a whole. It is because of Newton's work that we currently understand the effect of gravity on the earth as a global system. For instance, as a result of

Newton's investigation into the subject of gravity, we know today that geological features such as mountains and canyons can cause variances in the Earth's gravitational force. Newton must also be acknowledged for the realisation that the force of gravity becomes less robust as the distance from the equator diminishes, due to the rotation of the earth, as well as the declining mass and density of the planet from the equator to the poles.

Despite these accomplishments, Newton remained perplexed by the causes of the power implied by the variables of his mathematical equations on gravity. In other words, he was unable adequately to explain the natural forces upon which the power of gravity relied. Even though he tried to justify these forces by describing them merely as phenomena of nature, differing hypotheses on these phenomena still abound today.

SECTION D:

In 1915, Albert Einstein addressed Newton's reservations by developing the revolutionary theorem of general relativity. Einstein asserted that the paths of objects in motion can sometimes deviate, or change direction over the course of time, as a result of the curvature of spacetime. Numerous subsequent investigations into and tests of the theorem of general relativity have unequivocally supported Einstein's ground-breaking work.

Please go to the next page.

Tip: Questions 1 to 6 are multiple choice questions. Each one of the questions is asking for a specific detail from the passage. Scan each paragraph for keywords, quickly re-read the information in the paragraph, and then answer the question. Remember to select an answer, even if you are not confident about your choice. Even if you are not sure about the answer, you will have a 25% chance of being correct.

Questions 1 to 6

Choose the correct letter A, B, C or D.

1) According to the passage, what statement best describes Aristotle?
   A. He was the founder of the Law of Universal Gravitation
   B. He was best-known for producing error-free work.
   C. He was a famous Greek natural scientist.
   D. He was a contemporary of Ptolemy.

2) Descartes is celebrated for establishing what subject?
   A. mathematics
   B. natural science
   C. philosophy
   D. physics

3) According to the passage, which one of the following is true?
   A. Newton created his Law of Universal Gravitation immediately after he observed an apple falling from a tree in his orchard.

B. The Law of Universal Gravitation, while similar on occasion to falling apples, is usually the result of observing objects which descend more slowly to earth.

C. Newton's law of gravity was not the result of a single observation of a fruit tree, but rather was created over many years.

D. Stories about Newton's observance of falling apples are based on fact, rather than folklore, because of the time-consuming process of the theories relating to these stories.

4) All of the following key facts about gravity are mentioned in the passage EXCEPT

A. the effect of geology upon gravitational forces

B. the impact of the varying density of the earth on gravity

C. the manner in which gravitational force becomes weaker near the equator

D. the way in which gravity influences rock formations

5) Which one of the following phrases best explains the term general relativity?

A. changes in the motion of objects due to the curved path of spacetime

B. the inverse relationship between time and space

C. the proportionality between paths and objects

D. the manner in which later researchers supported Einstein

6) What can be inferred about the reaction of the scientific community to Einstein's theory of general relativity?

   A. It has received a mixed response.

   B. The response has been overwhelmingly positive.

   C. The reception has been mostly negative.

   D. The scientific community is still undecided about the value of Einstein's work.

Tip: Questions 7 to 9 are in the matching features format. You need to choose the main ideas from the list of statements provided. Skim through the passage again, and then choose the most general ideas from the list below. Also pay attention to how many sections or paragraphs from the passage discuss each idea. If more paragraphs are devoted to the topic, then it is much more likely to be a main topic, rather than a specific detail. Remember that you need to avoid points that are too specific.

Please go to the next page.

Questions 7 to 9

Select **THREE ANSWERS** from options A to F below that represent the most important ideas contained in the passage.

    A. The study of the mechanics of motion has endured for many centuries.

    B. Ptolemy is one of the most famous natural scientists.

    C. Newton's study of gravitational forces was of invaluable significance.

    D. The strength of gravitational force is directly related to the distance to the equator.

    E. Newton was confused by the power from which gravity was derived.

    F. Einstein's theorem of general relativity provided a much-needed development of Newton's work.

Tip: Questions 10 to 13 are in the matching headings format. Match a heading with the letter of each section from the passage. Matching headings questions are a type of main idea question. So, the heading or title needs to express the main idea of each section of the passage. Pay special attention to the assertions expressed in the first one or two sentences of each paragraph when answering these types of questions since the main idea of a paragraph is normally introduced in the first couple of sentences.

Questions 10-13

Reading passage 1 has 4 sections A to D. Choose the best heading for each section from the list of headings (i to viii) below.

List of Headings

i. Astronomy, philosophy and gravity

ii. The birth of gravitational theory

iii. Einstein: A modern-day genius

iv. General relativity and its supporters

v. Gravitational theory and the Renaissance

vi. Newton's work and its limitations

vii. The work of Aristotle

viii. Development of the law of universal gravitation

---

10) Section A _____

11) Section B _____

12) Section C _____

13) Section D _____

Please go to the next page.

READING PASSAGE 2

*You should spend about 20 minutes on **Questions 14 to 28** which are based on Reading Passage 2 below:*

Socio-economic Status

Socio-economic status, rather than intellectual ability, may be the key to a child's success later in life, according to a study by Carnegie. Let us consider two hypothetical primary school students named John and Paul. Both of these children work hard, pay attention in the classroom, and are respectful to their teachers. However, Paul's father is a prosperous business tycoon, while John's has a menial job working in a factory. Despite the similarities in their academic aptitudes, the disparate economic situations of their parents mean that Paul is nearly 30 times more likely than John to land a high-flying job by the time he reaches his fortieth year. In fact, John has only a 12% chance of finding and maintaining a job that would earn him even a median-level income.

Research dealing with the economics of inequality among adults supports these findings. Importantly, these studies also reveal that the economics of inequality is a trend that has become more and more pronounced in recent years. For instance, in the mid-twentieth century, the mean after-tax pay for a corporate executive (CEO) was more than 12 times that of the average factory worker. In 1975, the average CEO's pay had increased to 35 times that of a typical blue-collar worker. By 1980, the situation was even worse: the executive's wages and benefits were nearly 42 times that of the average wage of a factory worker. Today in the twenty-first century, this situation reached a level which some economists have called hyper-inequality. That is, it is common for the salary of the average executive to be more than 100 times that of the average factory employee. In fact, most CEOs are now making, on average, 530 times more than blue-collar employees.

Because of this and other economic dichotomies, a theoretical stance has recently sprung into existence, asserting that inequality is institutionalised. Simply stated, many researchers argue that workers from higher socio-economic backgrounds are disproportionately compensated, even though the contribution they make to society is no more valuable than that of their lower-paid counterparts. To rectify the present imbalance caused by this economic stratification, researchers claim that economic rewards should be judged by and distributed according to the worthiness of the employment to society as a whole. Economic rewards under this schema refer not only to wages or salaries, but also to power, status and prestige within one's community, as well as within larger society.

Recently, cultural and critical theorists have joined the economic debate that empirical researchers embarked upon decades ago. Focusing on the effect of cultural technologies and systems, they state that various forms of media promote the mechanisms of economic manipulation and oppression. Watching television, they claim, causes those of lower socio-economic class to view themselves as apolitical and powerless victims of the capitalistic machine. Of course, such a viewpoint has a deleterious impact upon individual identity and human motivation.

At a more personal level, economic inequality also has pervasive effects on the lives of the less economically fortunate. These personal effects include the manner in which one's economic status influences musical tastes, the perception of time and space, the expression of emotion and communication across social groups. The detrimental economic imbalance may at its most extreme form lead to differences in health and mortality in those from the lower economic levels of society.

While causing problems to many on a personal level, economic inequality is also of concern from a global perspective. The worldwide impact of economic inequality is so severe at present that certain poorer countries are considered to be peripheral in discussions of international monetary policy. In order to solve this problem, many economists believe that consideration must be given not only to political arrangements that make some groups more financially better off than others, but also to the social interaction between people and groups.

Conversely, other theorists argue that financial improvement does not always result in the betterment of any particular society. They point out that levels of personal happiness, as well as trust and cooperation between people, are often highest when monetary considerations within a group are kept to a minimum. Finally, they warn that judgements about any given nation's financial situation may be biased as a result of the Western emphasis on materialism and consumerism.

Please go to the next page.

> **Tip:** Questions 14 to 19 are in the summary completion format. Study the list of words below the summary. Then look for synonyms for these words in the passage. You should also pay special attention to sentence structure for questions like this. Ask yourself: Does the gap require a noun, verb, adjective or adverb? Then place the correct word in each gap.

Questions 14-19

*A summary of the first two paragraphs of the passage is given below. Complete the summary using words from the box. Use **ONLY ONE WORD** for each answer.*

Two **14)** .... students, John and Paul, can be used to illustrate **15)** .... disparities. Paul is from a(n) **16)** .... background, while John's family is poor. Even though both children perform well at school, Paul is ultimately much more likely to get a **17)** .... job than John. Research in the adult population is **18)** .... with this example. In recent years, the salaries of executives are much **19)** ...... than the wages of factory workers.

affluence	consistent	excessive	wealthy
higher	high-paying	imaginary	
social	society	usual	

> **Tip:** Questions 20 to 24 ask you to identify the writer's views. For each statement, scan the passage again to see if you can find each claim or argument. You need to look for antonyms and synonyms in the passage in order to answer questions like this one.

Questions 20-24

Do the following statements agree with the information in Reading Passage 2?

Write the following:

TRUE *if the statement agrees with the information in the passage*

FALSE *if the statement contradicts the information in the passage*

NOT GIVEN *if there is no information in the passage on this point*

20) Children from prosperous families are likely to remain affluent later in life.

21) The disparity between the rich and poor has lessened in recent years.

22) Blue-collar workers aspire to the lifestyles of CEOs.

23) Executives make a more valuable contribution to society than factory workers.

24) Economic rewards include both tangible and intangible factors.

Please go to the next page.

Tip: Questions 25 to 28 are in the gap fill format. Just like when you answer summary completion questions, you will first need to determine whether the gap requires a noun, verb, adjective or adverb before attempting to answer the question. A list of words is not provided for you, so you need to think of synonyms or derivatives of words from the passage and then place your word in each gap.

Questions 25-28

*Answer the questions below using **ONLY ONE WORD** for each answer.*

25) Media such as television may . . . . affect identity and motivation.

26) At its most extreme, social inequality may result in premature . . . .

27) During international monetary discussions, poor countries are often thought to be on the . . . .

28) However, social groups that do not focus on financial matters may be the most . . . .

READING PASSAGE 3

*You should spend about 20 minutes on **Questions 29 to 40** which are based on Reading Passage 3 below:*

A) Adventurers, fieldwork assistants and volunteers are gradually replacing tourists. Still, the classification 'tourist' will never totally disappear. There might still be those who wish to travel to foreign lands for their own enjoyment, but doing so will be a clandestine and frowned-upon activity. No one will admit to belonging to that category.

B) Burma and Bali have recently prohibited tourists from entering parts of their countries. The list of places that tourists cannot explore is ever expanding. The international tourist organisation Tourism Concern states that Belize, Botswana, China, East Africa, Peru, Thailand and Zanzibar all have areas that have been adversely impacted upon by tourism. Representatives from Tourism Concern believe that tourists are destroying the environment, as well as local cultures. These representatives also assert that although tourists bring money to the countries they visit, they must be stopped at any price.

C) These notions may seem ironic since tourism was unquestionably encouraged as something that was good a few decades ago. The advent of package holidays and charter flights meant that tourism could finally be enjoyed by the majority of the population. The year 1967 was declared "The International Year of the Tourist" by the United Nations, and by the end of the 1980s, tourism was the most profitable global industry. At the beginning of the twenty-first century, more than 20 million families a year were going abroad on holiday.

D) The World Tourism Organisation (WTO) has predicted that by the year 2050, there will be 1.56 billion tourists per year travelling somewhere in the world. This forecast demonstrates the immense challenge in trying to curb the global demand for tourism. In fact, the task may be so tremendous that it might just be impossible.

E) Some argue that the government should intervene, but the government alone would face huge impediments in attempting to make so many economically-empowered people stop doing something they enjoy. Others assert that tourism is of such extreme damage to the welfare of the world that only totally irresponsible individuals would ever even consider doing it. Yet, this argument is clearly absurd. Whatever benefits or otherwise accrue from tourism, it is not evil, despite what a tiny minority might say. It can cause harm. It can be neutral, and it can occasionally bring about something good.

F) As a result, tourism is under attack by more a more oblique method: it has been re-named. Bit by bit, the word "tourist" is being removed from what used to be called a "holiday" in the booklet that was once called a "holiday brochure".

G) Since tourism has changed, so too must the holiday. Adventurers, fieldwork assistants and volunteers do not go on holidays. These new travellers go on "cultural experiences", "expeditions" or "projects". However, re-branding tourism in this way gives freedom to travellers, as well as restrictions.

H) The various booklets, pamphlets and brochures distributed by the new industry for travellers are now attempting to emulate advertisements produced by charities. For example, *Global Adventure* magazine produces an annual "99 Great Adventures Guide" which mixes charitable expeditions with holidays as if the two things are one and the same.

I) New travellers express great interest in respecting the environments they visit. They avoid tourist infrastructures such as hotels because they are afraid of being viewed negatively by the local culture. Instead, they prefer accommodation arrangements such as cabins or camping. These types of accommodation, they believe, are more respectful of local culture. Local culture is very important to the new tourist, whereas the mass tourist is believed to destroy it.

J) Nevertheless, all types of tourism should be responsible towards and respectful of environmental and human resources. Some tourist developments, as well as individual tourists, have not acted with this in mind. Consequently, a divide is being driven between those few affluent and privileged tourists and the remaining majority. Our concern should be not with this small number of privileged people, but rather with the majority of travellers.

Tip: Question 29 asks you to select the best title for the passage. Questions that ask you to choose a title are just another type of main idea question. When answering questions about the main idea of a passage, remember to focus on the first paragraph since this is where the main idea of the passage is introduced.

Question 29

Choose the correct letter A, B, C or D.

29) What is the best title for this passage?

    A. Tourism and the Environment

    B. Adventurers, Tourists and Travellers

    C. The Changing Face of Tourism

    D. Tourism: Its Advantages and Disadvantages

Please go to the next page.

Tip: Questions 30 to 34 are in the form completion format. Scan the passage again for each idea or keyword provided in the form. Then think of a synonym of the word from the passage and place the synonym in the gap. Be sure to use the correct grammatical form.

Questions 30 to 34:

*Complete the chart below. Place **ONLY ONE WORD** in each gap.*

Year	Development in Tourism
1967	United Nations **30)** _____ tourism. Most people could finally **31)** _____ to go on holiday.
1980	Tourism industry experiences high **32)** _____
Today	In **33)** _____ of 700 million tourists each year.
2050	The WTO's **34)** _____ is that there will be 1.56 billion tourists at any time.

Please go to the next page.

> **Tip:** Questions 35 to 40 are in the identifying information format. For these types of questions, it is usually faster to search the passage in the order of the paragraphs, rather than trying to answer the questions in their order in the list below. If you scan from the list first, you will have to re-read information each time you refer back to the passage. So first, scan each paragraph, and underline the most important specific points. Then look at the list below and place the letter for that paragraph next to the statement.

Questions 35 to 40:

Now look at paragraphs E to J.

Which paragraph contains the following information?

Place one letter (E, F, G, H, I or J) in each gap.

35) The attack on tourism . . . .

36) An example of re-branding . . . .

37) An assertion for the reader's consideration . . . .

38) New tourism and the environment . . . .

39) Difficulties of governmental intervention . . . .

40) The pro's and con's of re-branding tourism . . . .

READING TEST 1 – ANSWER KEY

1) C

2) A

3) C

4) D

5) A

6) B

7 to 9) A, C, F

10) ii

11) v

12) vi

13) iv

14) imaginary

15) social

16) wealthy

17) high-paying

18) consistent

19) higher

20) T

21) F

22) NG

23) F

24) T

25) negatively / adversely

26) death

27) periphery / outside / margins

28) content / trustworthy / trusting / cooperative

29) C

30) supports

31) afford

32) profits / profitability / growth / demand

33) excess

34) prediction / forecast / estimate

35) F

36) H

37) J

38) I

39) E

40) G

READING TEST 1 – EXPLANATIONS TO THE ANSWERS

1) The correct answer is C. The keyword in this question is "Aristotle". We can see from scanning the passage that Aristotle is first mentioned in section A of the passage. The first paragraph tells us that Aristotle was "a Greek philosopher and natural scientist". The next sentence states: "In fact, most of Aristotle's life was devoted to the study of the objects of natural science, and it is for this work that he is most renowned". "Renowned" is synonymous with famous. Therefore, Aristotle can be best described as a famous Greek natural scientist.

2) The correct answer is A. The keyword in this question is "Descartes". We can see from scanning the passage that Descartes is mentioned in section B of the passage. The passage states: "Descartes . . . was known at that time as a dilettante philosopher, but was later dubbed the father of modern mathematics". "Dilettante" is used to describe a person who is not serious about his or her profession. "Dubbed" means to be named as something or to be acknowledged for something. So, Descartes is acknowledged as establishing the subject of mathematics.

3) The correct answer is C. If you are asked which answer is true or false, you need to read all of the answer choices and look for common keywords among options A to D. Here, we can see that the common

keywords are "Newton" and "gravitation". From scanning the text, we can see that "Newton" and "gravitation" are discussed in section C of the passage. Section C says: "While this finding, termed the Law of Universal Gravitation, is said to have been occasioned by Newton's observation of the fall of an apple from a tree in the orchard at his home, in reality, the idea did not come to the scientist in a flash of inspiration, but was developed slowly over time". This sentence is a paraphrase of answer C, which states: "Newton's law of gravity was not the result of a single observation of a fruit tree, but rather was created over many years." Note that "flash of inspiration" means an idea that comes to a person quickly or unexpectedly.

4) The correct answer is D. If you are asked which answer is not mentioned in the passage, you need to read all of the answer choices and rule each one out by the process of elimination. Answer A (the effect of geology upon gravitational forces) is mentioned in Section C, which states: "For instance, as a result of Newton's investigation into the subject of gravity, we know today that *geological features such as mountains and canyons can cause variances in the Earth's gravitational force*". Answer B (the impact of the varying density of the earth on gravity) is mentioned in the following sentence from section C: "Newton must also be

acknowledged for the realisation that the force of gravity becomes less robust as the distance from the equator diminishes, due to the rotation of the earth, as well as *the declining mass and density of the planet* from the equator to the poles". Answer C (the manner in which gravitational force becomes weaker near the equator) is also mentioned in the following sentence: "Newton must also be acknowledged for the realisation that *the force of gravity becomes less robust as the distance from the equator diminishes*, due to the rotation of the earth, as well as the declining mass and density of the planet from the equator to the poles". Answer D (the way in which gravity influences rock formations) is not mentioned in the passage.

5) The correct answer is A. The keyword for this question is "general relativity". We can see that this concept is explained in section D of the passage. General relativity is best explained as changes in the motion of objects due to the curved path of spacetime. The paragraph states: "Einstein asserted that the paths of objects in motion can sometimes deviate, or *change direction* over the course of time, as a result of the *curvature* of spacetime".

6) The correct answer is B. The reaction of the scientific community to Einstein's theory of general relativity has been overwhelmingly positive.

The last sentence states: "Numerous subsequent investigations into and tests of the theorem of general relativity have unequivocally supported Einstein's ground-breaking work". The adverb "unequivocally" and the adjective "ground-breaking" show that support of the theory has been overwhelmingly positive.

7 to 9)   The correct answers are: A, C and F. Remember that you need to look for the most important idea of each section of the passage in order to answer questions like this one. Answer A, which states that the study of the mechanics of motion has endured for many centuries, is a summary of section A of the passage. We know that this is the most important idea of section A because the section begins with this assertion: "The question of the mechanics of motion is complex and one that has a protracted history. Indeed, much has been discovered about gravity, defined as the force that draws objects to the earth, both *before and since . . . the 17th century*". Answer C, which states that Newton's study of gravitational forces was of invaluable significance, is a summary of section C. We know that this is the most important idea of section C because the section states: "Newton had the prescience to appreciate that *his study was of great import for the scientific community and for society as a whole*. It is because of Newton's work that we currently understand the effect of

gravity on the earth as a global system". Answer F, which states that Einstein's theorem of general relativity provided a much-needed development of Newton's work, is the main idea of section D. We know that this is the most important idea of section D because the section begins as follows: "In 1915, Albert Einstein *addressed Newton's reservations* by developing the *revolutionary theorem* of general relativity".

10) The correct answer is ii. Heading questions are just another type of main idea question. The main idea of section A is the birth of gravitational theory. Section A gives the historical background to the theory and explains some of its important foundational discoveries.

11) The correct answer is v. The main idea of section B is gravitational theory and the Renaissance. The first sentence in this section states: "It was during the period called the Renaissance that gravitational forces were perhaps studied most widely".

12) The correct answer is vi. The main idea of section C is Newton's work and its limitations. The first sentence in this section states: "Newton took these studies a step further". We learn about the limitations later in the paragraph: "Newton remained perplexed by the causes of the power implied by the variables of his mathematical equations on gravity".

13) The correct answer is iv. The main idea of section D is general relativity and its supporters. The first sentence in this section states: "In 1915, Albert Einstein addressed Newton's reservations by developing the revolutionary theorem of general relativity". We know that the theory has supporters because it is described as "revolutionary".

14) The correct answer is "imaginary". We know that the gap requires an adjective because the word after the gap is a noun, so the gap is placed within a noun phrase. The passage states: "Let us consider two hypothetical primary school students named John and Paul. Both of these children work hard, pay attention in the classroom, and are respectful to their teachers". "Imaginary" and "hypothetical" are synonyms.

15) The correct answer is "social". We know that the gap requires an adjective because the word after the gap is a noun. The passage describes socio-economic status and the economics of inequality. Inequality and disparity are synonyms, and social and socio-economic are similar in meaning, although they are not exact synonyms.

16) The correct answer is "wealthy". We know that the gap requires another adjective because the word after the gap is a noun. The passage tells us that "Paul's father is a prosperous business tycoon". Prosperous and wealthy are synonyms. You may be tempted to choose the word

"affluence". However, this is not the correct answer because it is a noun, and we need an adjective in the gap.

17) The correct answer is "high-paying". The passage tells us that "Paul is nearly 30 times more likely than John to land a high-flying job by the time he reaches his fortieth year". High-paying and high-flying are synonyms in this context.

18) The correct answer is "consistent". "Consistent" is the only adjective from the list that takes the preposition "with". In addition, the first sentence of paragraph two states: "Research dealing with the economics of inequality among adults supports these findings". "Consistent with" and "support" are synonyms.

19) The correct answer is "higher". Near the end of paragraph two, we learn that "it is now common for the salary of the average executive to be more than 100 times that of the average factory employee". The phrase "more than 100 times" is similar to the phrase "much higher than".

20) The correct answer is T. The first paragraph provides the following specific example: "Paul's father is a prosperous business tycoon, while John's has a menial job working in a factory. Despite the similarities in their academic aptitudes, the disparate economic situations of their parents mean that Paul is nearly 30 times more likely than John to land a

high-flying job by the time he reaches his fortieth year". From this specific example, we can induce the general assertion that "children from prosperous families are likely to remain affluent later in life".

21) The correct answer is F. The question asserts that "the disparity between the rich and poor has lessened in recent years". This assertion is false because paragraph two tells us: "By 1980, the situation was even worse: the executive's wages and benefits were nearly 42 times that of the average wage of a factory worker. Today in the twenty-first century, this situation reached a level which some economists have called hyper-inequality. That is, it is common for the salary of the average executive to be more than 100 times that of the average factory employee. In fact, most CEOs are now making, on average, 530 times more than blue-collar employees".

22) The correct answer is NG. The question asserts that "Blue-collar workers aspire to the lifestyles of CEOs". The passage talks about the differences in earnings between the two groups. However, the passage does not mention the aspirations or ambitions of blue-collar workers.

23) The correct answer is F. The question asserts that "executives make a more valuable contribution to society than factory workers". This assertion is false because paragraph three states: "Workers from higher socio-

economic backgrounds are disproportionately compensated, even though the contribution they make to society is no more valuable than that of their lower-paid counterparts". The phrase "lower-paid counterparts" refers to factory workers.

24) The correct answer is T. The question asserts that "economic rewards include both tangible and intangible factors". This assertion is true because the last sentence of paragraph three states that "economic rewards under this schema refer not only to wages or salaries, but also to power, status and prestige within one's community, as well as within larger society". Wages and salaries are tangible factors, while power, status and prestige are intangible factors.

25) Possible correct answers are: negatively / adversely. We know that the gap needs an adverb because the word after the gap is a verb. The passage states: "Watching television, they claim, causes those of lower socio-economic class to view themselves as apolitical and powerless victims of the capitalistic machine. Of course, such a viewpoint has a deleterious impact upon individual identity and human motivation". The phrase "has a deleterious impact" from the passage and the phrase "negatively or adversely affect" from the answer are synonyms.

26) The correct answer is "death". We know that the gap needs a noun because the word before the gap is an adjective. The passage states: "The detrimental economic imbalance may at its most extreme form lead to differences in health and mortality in those from the lower economic levels of society". The word "mortality" from the passage and the word "death" from the answer are synonyms.

27) Possible correct answers are: periphery / outside / margins. The word in the gap needs to be a noun because the word before the gap is an article. Paragraph six states: "The worldwide impact of economic inequality is so severe at present that certain poorer countries are considered to be peripheral in discussions of international monetary policy". The phrase "are considered to be peripheral" from the passage and the phrase "thought to be on the periphery" from the answer are synonymous. In other words, you need to change the adjective "peripheral" to the noun "periphery" in order to answer the question. Alternatively, you may use "outside" or "margins", which are synonymous with "periphery".

28) Possible correct answers are: content / trustworthy / trusting / cooperative. An adjective must be placed in the gap because the gap is preceded by the word "most". The last paragraph states: "Conversely,

other theorists argue that financial improvement does not always result in the betterment of any particular society. They point out that levels of personal *happiness*, as well as *trust* and *cooperation* between people, are often highest when monetary considerations within a group are kept to a minimum". So, the passage mentions the following characteristics of social groups: happiness, trust and cooperation. We cannot use the word "happy" in the gap because the superlative form of this adjective is "happiest". So, the possible adjectives are: content, trustworthy, trusting or cooperative.

29) The correct answer is C. The best title for the passage is "The Changing Face of Tourism". The first sentence of the passage states: "Adventurers, fieldwork assistants and volunteers are gradually replacing tourists". This sentence introduces the idea of changes to tourism, and these changes are explained in depth in the passage.

30) The correct answer is "supports". We are looking for the keywords "United Nations" as well as the year 1967, which are mentioned in paragraph C. Paragraph C states: "The year 1967 was declared 'The International Year of the Tourist' by the United Nations". We need a verb to make the phrase grammatically correct, so the verb "supports" can be placed in the gap.

31) The correct answer is "afford". We again need to refer to paragraph C for the year 1967. That paragraph states: "The advent of package holidays and charter flights meant that tourism could finally be enjoyed by the majority of the population". Package holidays and charter flights are low-cost holidays. Since we need to put a verb in the gap and we are talking about the cost of something, the word "afford" is the best answer.

32) Possible correct answers are: profits / profitability / growth / demand. Scan the passage for the year 1980. We can see that this year is also discussed in paragraph C, which explains: "by the end of the 1980s, tourism was the most profitable global industry". We need to put a noun in the gap because the gap is preceded by the adjective "high". So, possible answers are: profits, profitability, growth or demand.

33) The correct answer is "excess". The last sentence of paragraph C states: "At the beginning of the twenty-first century, more than 20 million families a year were going abroad on holiday". If we assume that each family consists of three or four people, we can estimate the total amount as 700 million tourists. The phrase "more than" from the passage and the phrase "in excess of" from the answer are synonyms.

34) Possible correct answers are: prediction / forecast / estimate. Scan the passage for the year 2050 and the keyword "WTO". We can see that

these ideas are discussed in paragraph D as follows: "The World Tourism Organisation (WTO) has predicted that by the year 2050, there will be 1.56 billion tourists per year traveling somewhere in the world". We know that we need a noun in the gap because the gap is preceded by the possessive form. The verb "predicted" from the passage can therefore be changed to the noun "prediction" for our answer. "Forecast" and "estimate" are synonymous with "prediction", so they are also possible answers.

35) The correct answer is F. The attack on tourism is mentioned in the first sentence of paragraph F as follows: "As a result, tourism is under attack by more a more oblique method: it has been re-named".

36) The correct answer is H. An example of re-branding is mentioned in paragraph H. We can find this example in the following sentence: "The various booklets, pamphlets and brochures distributed by the new industry for travellers are now attempting to emulate advertisements produced by charities".

37) The correct answer is J. An assertion for the reader's consideration is mentioned in paragraph J. The last paragraph of the passage ends with the following assertion for the reader's consideration: "Our concern

should be not with this small number of privileged people, but rather with the majority of travellers".

38) The correct answer is I. New tourism and the environment are mentioned in paragraph I. We can see this from the first sentence of paragraph I, which states: "New travellers express great interest in respecting the environments they visit".

39) The correct answer is E. Difficulties of governmental intervention are mentioned in the first sentence of paragraph E: "Some argue that the government should intervene, but the government alone would face huge impediments in attempting to make so many economically-empowered people stop doing something they enjoy".

40) The correct answer is G. The pro's and con's of re-branding tourism are mentioned in in the last sentence of paragraph G, which states: "However re-branding tourism in this way gives freedom to travellers, as well as restrictions". The freedom is the pro (or the advantage) and the restrictions are the con (or the disadvantage).

IELTS Practice Reading – Test 2
Answer Sheet

1. 21.
2. 22.
3. 23.
4. 24.
5. 25.
6. 26.
7. 27.
8. 28.
9. 29.
10. 30.
11. 31.
12. 32.
13. 33.
14. 34.
15. 35.
16. 36.
17. 37.
18. 38.
19. 39.
20. 40.

IELTS Practice Reading – Test 2

READING PASSAGE 1

*You should spend about 20 minutes on **Questions 1 to 14** which are based on Reading Passage 1 below:*

Tornadoes are one of the most severe types of weather phenomena. While many people fear tornadoes and their destructive power, few people understand their real causes and effects, nor are they aware of how to protect themselves from their devastating force.

Tornadoes, violently rotating columns of air, occur when a change in wind direction, coupled with an increase in wind speed, results in a spinning effect in the lower atmosphere. These whirling movements, which may not be visible to the naked eye, are exacerbated when the rotating air column shifts from a horizontal to a vertical position. As the revolving cloud draws in the warm air that surrounds it at ground level, its spinning motion begins to accelerate, thereby creating a funnel that extends from the cloud above it to the ground below. In this way, tornadoes become pendent from low pressure storm clouds.

When a tornado comes into contact with the ground, it produces a strong upward draft known as a vortex, a spiralling column of wind that can reach speeds in excess of 200 miles per hour. Travelling across the landscape, the tornado wreaks a path of concentrated destruction. It is not uncommon for these twisters to lift heavy objects, like cars or large animals, and throw them several miles. Houses that succumb to the force of the tornado seem to explode as the low air pressure inside the vortex collides with the normal air pressure inside the buildings.

Tornadoes can occur at any time of the year, but are typically most frequent during the summer months. Equally, tornadoes can happen at any time during the day, but usually occur between 3:00 in the afternoon and 9:00 in the evening. While these fierce funnels occur in many parts of the world, they are most common in the United States. On average, there are 1,200 tornadoes per year in this vast nation, causing 70 fatalities and 1,500 injuries.

Although taking myriad shapes and sizes, tornadoes are generally categorised as weak, strong, or violent. The majority of all tornadoes are classified as weak, meaning that their duration is less than 10 minutes and they have a speed under 110 miles per hour. Comprising approximately 10 percent of all twisters, strong tornadoes may last for more than 20 minutes and reach speeds up to 205 miles per hour. Violent tornadoes are the rarest, occurring less than one percent of the time. While uncommon, tornadoes in this classification are the most devastating, lasting more than one hour and resulting in the greatest loss of life. Even though only violent tornadoes can completely destroy a well-built, solidly-constructed home, weaker ones can also cause great damage.

Owing to the powerful and destructive nature of these whirling funnel clouds, there are, perhaps not surprisingly, a number of myths and misconceptions surrounding them. For instance, many people mistakenly believe that tornadoes never occur over rivers, lakes, and oceans; yet, waterspouts, tornadoes that form over bodies of water, often move onshore and cause extensive damage to coastal areas. In addition, tornadoes can accompany hurricanes and tropical storms as they move to land. Another common myth about tornadoes is that damage to erected structures, like houses and office buildings, can be avoided if windows are opened prior to the impact of the storm. Based on the misunderstanding that open windows might equalise the pressure inside the structure and minimise the damage to it, this action can instead result in fatal injury.

Because of the profound effects that tornadoes have on communities and their inhabitants, safety measures are of paramount importance during adverse weather conditions. Drivers often attempt to outrun tornadoes in their cars, but it is extremely unsafe to do so. Automobiles offer very little protection when twisters strike, so drivers should abandon their vehicles and seek safe shelter. Mobile homes afford little shelter, so residents of these homes should go to an underground floor of the sturdiest nearby building. In the case of a building having no underground area, a person should go to the lowest floor of the building and place him or herself under a piece of heavy furniture. If no building is available, a person caught in a tornado should lie prostate in a nearby ditch or other depressed area of land and cover his or her head.

Please go to the next page.

Questions 1 to 7

Do the following statements agree with the claims of the writer of Reading Passage 1?

Write the following:

TRUE   if the statement agrees with the information in the passage

FALSE   if the statement contradicts the information in the passage

NOT GIVEN   if there is no information in the passage on this point

1) The public generally understands what safety measures to adopt in the event of a tornado.

2) Tornadoes are triggered by two simultaneous weather conditions.

3) Tornado speed has increased in recent years.

4) The likelihood of a tornado is greatest during the early morning hours.

5) The possibility of tornado damage can be mitigated by ensuring that a structure has been well constructed.

6) Tornadoes and hurricanes are more frequent in-land than in coastal areas.

7) The safest place for a person to be during a tornado is in a basement.

Questions 8 to 13

Answer the questions below using **NO MORE THAN FOUR WORDS** for each answer.

8) The tornado begins to develop as it gathers warm air from what area of the atmosphere?

　　　..

9) During which part of the year are tornadoes most frequent?

　　　..

10) What types of objects can tornadoes hurl over long distances?

　　　..

11) What is the average duration of a weak tornado?

　　　..

12) Which category of tornadoes are the least common?

　　　..

13) What should a person do if he or she is in a vehicle when a tornado occurs?

　　　..

Question 14

Choose the correct letter A, B, C, D or E.

14) What is the best title for reading passage 1?

   A. Tornadoes: Facts and Fiction

   B. Tornadoes: Causes and Effects

   C. Tornadoes and Personal Safety

   D. Tornadoes: Recent Research

   E. Tornadoes: Myths and Misconceptions

Please go to the next page.

READING PASSAGE 2

*You should spend about 20 minutes on **Questions 15 to 27** which are based on Reading Passage 2 below:*

Jean Piaget

Born in France in 1896, Jean Piaget became one of the most influential thinkers in the areas of education psychology and child development in the twentieth and twenty-first centuries. The primary thrust of his research revolved around the question: "How do human beings come to know?" His research culminated in the ground-breaking discovery of what he called "abstract symbolic reasoning". The basic idea behind this principle was that biology influences child development to a greater extent than does socialisation. That is to say, Piaget concluded that younger children answered research questions differently than older ones not because they were less intelligent, but because their intelligence was at a lower stage of biological development.

Because he was a biologist, Piaget had a keen interest in the adaptation of organisms to their environment, and this preoccupation led to many astute observations. Piaget found that behaviour in children was controlled by mental organisations called "schemes," which enable an individual to interpret his or her world and respond to situations. Piaget coined the term "equilibration" to describe the biological need of human beings to balance these schemes against the processes of environmental adaptation.

The French-born biologist postulated that schemes are innate since all children are born with these drives. Noting that while other animals continued to deploy their in-born schemes throughout the entire duration of their lives, Piaget hypothesised that human beings' pre-existing, innate schemes compete with, and ultimately diverge from, constructed schemes, which are socially-acquired in the environmental adaptation process.

Being of central significance to Piaget's project, the concept of adaptation can be bifurcated into two discrete functions: assimilation and accommodation. The first of these refers to the process of transforming one's environment in order to bring about its conformance to innate cognitive schemes and structures. Alternatively, the latter function describes the changing of pre-existing schemes or mental structures in order to accept the conditions of one's environment. For instance, schemes used in infant breast feeding and bottle feeding are examples of assimilation because the child utilises his or her innate capacity for sucking to complete both tasks. On the other hand, when the child starts to eat from a spoon instead of a bottle, he or she undergoes the process of accommodation since a completely new method of consuming food must be learned.

As Piaget's research with children progressed, he identified four stages of cognitive development. In the first stage, which he termed the sensorimotor stage, Piaget noted that at the incipience of the child's mental development, intelligence is displayed by way of the infant's physical interactions with the world. That is, the child's intelligence is directly correlated to his or her mobility and motor activity. Infants begin to develop some language skills, as well as memory, which Piaget called "object permanence," during this initial stage.

When the child becomes a toddler, he or she enters the pre-operational stage. During this stage the child is largely egocentric, meaning that intellectual and emotional energy is directed inwardly, rather than toward other individuals. Although memory, language, and intelligence continue to develop during these years, thinking is illogical and inflexible on the whole.

Next, the child begins the concrete operational stage. Beginning roughly at age five, this stage is characterised by the appearance of logical and systematic thought processes. In this stage, the child begins to conceptualise symbols and measurements relating to concrete objects, such as numbers, weights, lengths, and volumes. As the child's intelligence becomes more logical, egocentrism begins to dissipate.

At the commencement of the teenage years, the final stage, called the formal operational stage, is initiated. During this stage, the individual should be able to grasp abstract thought on a range of complex ideas and theories. Unfortunately, recent research has shown that adults in many countries around the globe have failed to complete this stage, perhaps owing to poverty or poor educational opportunities.

Please go to the next page.

Questions 15-20

Choose the correct letter A, B, C or D.

15) Based on the information in paragraph 1, which of the following best explains the term abstract symbolic reasoning?

   A. The idea that younger children are less intelligent that older children.

   B. The idea that younger children are less physically developed than older children.

   C. The idea that younger children are less socially developed than older children.

   D. The idea that biological development affects the intellectual development of children.

16) All of the following are accurate statements about Piaget EXCEPT

   A. Piaget's views as a biologist affected his work on child development.

   B. Piaget discovered that the child's biological development is connected to his or her mental functioning.

   C. Piaget noted that environmental factors, as well as biological factors, played a role in child development.

   D. Piaget was the first scientist to investigate child development.

17) According to the passage, which one of the following statements is true?
   A. Piaget theorised that, unlike the schemes of other animals, human beings' schemes are primarily acquired in the socialisation process.
   B. In contrast to other animals, human beings use their innate schemes throughout their lifetimes, rather than departing from constructed schemes.
   C. The process by which human beings acquire schemes is different than that of other animals because human beings acquire schemes during the socialisation process, and these acquired schemes bifurcate from their innate schemes.
   D. Piaget noted that human beings differ to other animals since humans do not rely only on in-born cognitive mechanisms.

18) According to the passage, which of the following statements best characterises the sensorimotor stage?
   A. The growth of the child's intelligence in this stage depends predominantly on his or her verbal ability.
   B. The skills obtained during this stage are of less importance than those achieved during later developmental stages.
   C. During this stage, the child learns how his or her mobility relates to language.
   D. The child's cognitive development in this stage is achieved through physical movement in his or her environment.

19) Based on the information in paragraphs 6 and 7, what can be inferred about child development?

   A. Before the child enters the concrete operational stage, his or her thinking is largely rigid and unsystematic.
   B. The conceptualisation of symbols is not as important as the conceptualisation of numbers.
   C. The child becomes more egocentric during the concrete operational stage.
   D. Memory and language before less important during the concrete operational stage.

20) According to the passage, the formal operational stage

   A. is the result of poor economic conditions.
   B. has not yet been finished by many individuals around the world.
   C. is an important global problem.
   D. in no way is connected to the availability of education.

Please go to the next page.

Questions 21 to 27

*Complete the chart below, using **ONLY ONE WORD** for each gap.*

Stage	Age	Skill Development	Comments
Sensorimotor	infant	motor activity	"Object permanence" and the **21)** _____ of language skills
Pre-operational	**22)** _____	memory, language, intelligence	Thought processes are characterised by lack of: **23)** _____ and **24)** _____
Concrete operational	5 to 12 years old	logic, conceptualisation	The child becomes less **25)** _____
Formal operational	**26)** _____	**27)** _____ thinking	Adults in poor countries may not reach this stage.

READING PASSAGE 3

*You should spend about 20 minutes on **Questions 28 to 40** which are based on Reading Passage 3 below:*

[1] The discipline of archaeology has been developing since wealthy European men began to plunder relics from distant lands in the early nineteenth century. Initially considered an upper-class hobby, archaeology in general and archaeological field methods in particular have undergone many developments and experienced many challenges in recent years.

[2] Before the field excavation begins, a viable site must first be located. While this process can involve assiduous research, sometimes sheer luck or an archaeologist's instinctive hunch also come into play. A logical locality to begin searching is one near sites in which artefacts have been found previously. Failing that, an archaeologist must consider, at a minimum, whether the potential site would have been habitable for people in antiquity. Bearing in mind that modern conveniences and facilities like electricity and running water were not available in pre-historic times, the archaeologist quickly discerns that sites near rivers and caves could provide the water and shelter indispensable for day-to-day living in such inhospitable conditions.

[3] Once the site has been located, the process of surveying commences. This means that the ground surface of the site is visually scrutinised to determine whether any artefacts are protruding through the soil. The archaeologist then digs test pits, small holes that are equidistant to one another, to determine what the boundaries of the larger final pit will be.

Once these dimensions are determined, the hole is dug and sectioned off with rope or plastic.

[4] The excavation, which is a meticulous and lengthy process, then begins in full. The archaeologist must gauge the texture and colour of the soil carefully as the pit becomes deeper and deeper since variations in soil composition can be used to identify climatic and other living conditions. It is imperative that the walls of the excavation are kept uniformly straight as the dig progresses so that these differences can be identified.

[5] The soil that is removed from the pit is sifted through a sieve or similar device, consisting of a screen that is suspended across a metal or wooden frame. After the soil is placed in the sieve, the archaeologist gently oscillates the device. As the mechanism goes back and forth in this way, the soil falls to the ground below, while larger objects are caught in the screen.

[6] Throughout this process, all findings are entered in a written record to ensure that every artefact is catalogued. This activity can certainly be tedious; yet, it is one that is critical in order to account for each and every item properly. Each finding is placed in a plastic bag bearing a catalogue number. Subsequent to this, a map of the excavation site is produced, on which the exact in-situ location of every artefact is indicated by level and position.

[7] Finally, the arduous task of interpreting the findings ensues. During the last two centuries, various approaches have been utilised in this respect. Throughout the early 1800s, most fossil recovery took place on the European continent, resulting in an extremely Euro-centric method of

examination and dissemination of findings. Unfortunately, as a consequence, the misapprehension that the origins of homosapiens were European began to take shape both in the archaeological and wider communities.

[8] Recent research suggests that inherent social and cultural biases pervaded the manner in which archaeological findings were investigated and explicated during the early nineteenth century because little attention was paid to the roles that wealth, status and nationality played in the interpretation of the artefacts. These problems began to be surmounted, however, in the 1860s, which witnessed the advent of the theories of Charles Darwin on the origin of the human species.

[9] Darwinian theory, the notion that human beings are the ultimate product of a long biological evolutionary process, then infiltrated the discipline of archaeology and heavily influenced the manner in which archaeological artefacts were recovered and analysed. By the middle of the 1900s, the imbalance created by the cultural biases began to be rectified as there was a surge in artefacts excavated from African and Asian localities.

Please go to the next page.

Questions 28 to 33

Reading Passage 3 has nine paragraphs. Which paragraph contains the following information?

Place one number in each gap.

28) Discovering the artefacts . . . .

29) Preparation of the site . . . .

30) Analysis of findings . . . .

31) Selection of a suitable venue . . . .

32) Cataloguing the objects . . . .

33) Monitoring the digging process . . . .

Please go to the next page.

Questions 34 to 40

A summary of the last two paragraphs of the passage is given below. Complete the summary using words from the box provided after the passage.

Use **ONLY ONE WORD** for each answer.

Research indicates that the interpretation of archaeological artefacts discovered in the early nineteenth century may have been **34)** .... That is because **35)** .... was not given to the effect of affluence and nationality on the **36)** .... of the artefacts. However, by the mid-1900s, **37)** .... theory, established by Charles Darwin, began to have a(n) **38)** .... on the examination of artefacts. Then, the problems caused by cultural **39)** .... started to be overcome. As a result, an increasing **40)** .... of artefacts were recovered from Africa and Asia at that time.

amount	analysis	biased
consideration	comments	Darwin
evolutionary	impact	plunder
prejudice	rectified	

READING TEST 2 – ANSWER KEY

1) F

2) T

3) NG

4) F

5) T

6) NG

7) T

8) (at) ground level

9) (the) summer months

10) cars / large animals / houses

11) less than 10 minutes

12) violent / violent tornadoes

13) abandon their vehicles / abandon the vehicles / seek safe shelter

14) A

15) D

16) D

17) C

18) D

19) A

20) B

21) development

22) toddler

23) logic

24) flexibility

25) selfish / egocentric

26) teenage / teenager

27) abstract

28) 5

29) 3

30) 7

31) 2

32) 6

33) 4

34) biased

35) consideration

36) analysis

37) evolutionary

38) impact

39) prejudice

40) amount

READING TEST 2 – EXPLANATIONS TO THE ANSWERS

1) The correct answer is F. The assertion in the question states: The public generally understands what safety measures to adopt in the event of a tornado. This assertion is false because paragraph 1 says that "few people understand their real causes and effects, nor are they aware of how to protect themselves from their devastating force".

2) The correct answer is T. The assertion in the question states: Tornadoes are triggered by two simultaneous weather conditions. This assertion is true because paragraph 2 says that "tornadoes . . . occur when a change in wind direction, coupled with an increase in wind speed, results in a spinning effect in the lower atmosphere".

3) The correct answer is NG. The assertion in the question states: Tornado speed has increased in recent years. Paragraph 3 mentions the possible maximum speed or tornadoes, but it does not mention whether the speed has increased recently.

4) The correct answer is F. The assertion in the question states: The likelihood of a tornado is greatest during the early morning hours. This assertion is false because paragraph 4 says that "tornadoes can happen at any time during the day, but usually occur between 3:00 in the afternoon and 9:00 in the evening".

5) The correct answer is T. The assertion in the question states: The possibility of tornado damage can be mitigated by ensuring that a structure has been well constructed. This assertion is true because the last sentence of paragraph 5 says that "only violent tornadoes can completely destroy a well-built, solidly-constructed home".

6) The correct answer is NG. The assertion in the question states: Tornadoes and hurricanes are more frequent in-land than in coastal areas. Paragraph 6 says that "tornadoes can accompany hurricanes and tropical storms as they move to land". However, the passage does not comment on the frequency of hurricanes.

7) The correct answer is T. The assertion in the question states: The safest place for a person to be during a tornado is in a basement. This assertion is true because the last paragraph says: "Mobile homes afford little shelter, so residents of these homes should go to an underground floor of the sturdiest nearby building. In the case of a building having no underground area, a person should go to the lowest floor of the building and place him or herself under a piece of heavy furniture". The basement is the underground floor of a house or other building.

8) The correct answer is: (at) ground level. Paragraph 2 states: "As the revolving cloud draws in the warm air that surrounds it *at ground level*, its spinning motion begins to accelerate".

9) The correct answer is: (the) summer months. Paragraph 4 states: "Tornadoes can occur at any time of the year, but are typically most frequent during *the summer months*".

10) Possible correct answers are: cars / large animals / houses. Paragraph 3 states: "It is not uncommon for these twisters to lift heavy objects, like *cars* or *large animals*, and throw them several miles. *Houses* that succumb to the force of the tornado seem to explode as the low air pressure inside the vortex collides with the normal air pressure inside the buildings".

11) The correct answer is "less than 10 minutes". Paragraph 5 states: "The majority of all tornadoes are classified as weak, meaning that their duration is *less than 10 minutes*".

12) Possible correct answers are: violent / violent tornadoes. Paragraph 5 also states: "*Violent tornadoes* are the rarest, occurring less than one percent of the time".

13) Possible correct answers are: abandon their vehicles / abandon the vehicles / seek safe shelter. The last paragraph states: "Automobiles

offer very little protection when twisters strike, so drivers should abandon their vehicles and seek safe shelter".

14) The correct answer is A. The best title for the passage is "Tornadoes: Facts and Fiction". The first five paragraphs of the passage give facts and statistics about tornadoes. In paragraph 6, "myths and misconceptions" (in other words, fictional ideas about tornadoes) are mentioned. Paragraphs 7 and 8 give facts about tornado safety.

15) The correct answer is D. Based on the information in paragraph 1, the best explanation of the term abstract symbolic reasoning is the idea that biological development affects the intellectual development of children. Paragraph 1 states: "His research culminated in the ground-breaking discovery of what he called 'abstract symbolic reasoning' . . . Piaget concluded that younger children answered research questions differently than older ones not because they were less intelligent, but because their intelligence was at a lower stage of biological development". Because of the emphasis on biological development in paragraph 1, we know that "intellectual development" and "intelligence" are synonymous in this context.

16) The correct answer is D. The statement that "Piaget was the first scientist to investigate child development" is not mentioned in the

passage. The first sentence of the passage states: "Jean Piaget became one of the most influential thinkers in the areas of education psychology and child development in the twentieth and twenty-first centuries". However, the passage does not imply that Piaget was the first researcher in this area.

17) The correct answer is C. It is true that the process by which human beings acquire schemes is different than that of other animals because human beings acquire schemes during the socialisation process, and these acquired schemes bifurcate from their innate schemes. Paragraph 3 states: "Noting that while other animals continued to deploy their in-born schemes throughout the entire duration of their lives, Piaget hypothesised that human beings' pre-existing, innate schemes compete with, and ultimately diverge from, constructed schemes, which are socially-acquired in the environmental adaptation process". "Bifurcate" and "diverge from" are synonyms in this context.

18) The correct answer is D. The statement that best characterises the sensorimotor stage is that the child's cognitive development is achieved through physical movement in his or her environment. Paragraph 5 states: "In the first stage, which he termed the sensorimotor stage, Piaget noted that at the incipience of the child's mental development, intelligence

is displayed by way of *the infant's physical interactions with the world*. That is, the child's intelligence is directly correlated to his or her mobility and motor activity".

19) The correct answer is A. Based on the information in paragraphs 6 and 7, the reader can infer the following: Before the child enters the concrete operational stage, his or her thinking is largely rigid and unsystematic. Paragraph 6 states that "although memory, language and intelligence continue to develop during these years, thinking is *illogical* and *inflexible* on the whole", and paragraph 7 adds that "the child begins the concrete operational stage . . . [which is] characterised by the appearance of *logical* and *systematic* thought processes." If the child's thoughts become logical and systematic in the concrete operational stage, we can surmise the child's thoughts are not logical and systematic before this stage.

20) The correct answer is B. According to the passage, the formal operational stage has not yet been finished by many individuals around the world. The last sentence of the passage explains that "recent research has shown that adults in many countries around the globe have failed to complete this stage, perhaps owing to poverty or poor educational opportunities".

21) The correct answer is "development". "Object permanence" and the *development* of language skills take place during the sensorimotor stage. Paragraph 5 states: "Infants begin to develop some language skills, as well as memory, which Piaget called 'object permanence,' during this initial stage.

22) The correct answer is "toddler". During the pre-operational stage, the child is a *toddler*. The first sentence of paragraph 6 states: "When the child becomes a toddler, he or she enters the pre-operational stage".

23 and 24) The correct answers are: "logic" and "flexibility". Thought processes are characterised by lack of *logic* and *flexibility* in the pre-operational stage. Paragraph 6 states: "Although memory, language, and intelligence continue to develop during these years, thinking is illogical and inflexible on the whole".

25) Possible correct answers are: selfish / egocentric. The child becomes less *selfish* or *egocentric* during the concrete operational stage. Paragraph 7 states: "As the child's intelligence becomes more logical, egocentrism begins to dissipate". "Dissipate" means to disappear.

26) Possible correct answers are: teenage / teenager. The formal operational stage takes place when the individual is a *teenager*. The last

paragraph states: "At the commencement of the teenage years, the final stage, called the formal operational stage, is initiated".

27) The correct answer is "abstract". The skill of *abstract* thought is developed during the formal operational stage. The last paragraph also states that "during this stage, the individual should be able to grasp abstract thought on a range of complex ideas and theories".

28) The correct answer is 5. Discovering the artefacts is mentioned in paragraph 5. The paragraph states: "As the mechanism goes back and forth in this way, the soil falls to the ground below, while larger objects are caught in the screen". The larger objects that are revealed are the artefacts.

29) The correct answer is 3. Preparation of the site is mentioned in paragraph 3. The paragraph states: "The archaeologist then digs test pits, small holes that are equidistant to one another, to determine what the boundaries of the larger final pit will be. Once these dimensions are determined, the hole is dug and sectioned off with rope or plastic". We know that the digging of these holes consists of preparation of the site because the next paragraph begins as follows: "The excavation, which is a meticulous and lengthy process, then begins in full". In other words,

since the excavation is the beginning, the steps that precede it are the preparation.

30) The correct answer is 7. Analysis of findings is mentioned in paragraph 7. The paragraph begins as follows: "Finally, the arduous task of interpreting the findings ensues".

31) The correct answer is 2. Selection of a suitable venue is mentioned in paragraph 2. The paragraph states: "Before the field excavation begins, a viable site must first be located".

32) The correct answer is 6. Cataloguing the objects is mentioned in paragraph 6. The paragraph states: "Throughout this process, all findings are entered in a written record to ensure that every artefact is catalogued".

33) The correct answer is 4. Monitoring the digging process is mentioned in paragraph 4. The paragraphs states: "The archaeologist must gauge the texture and colour of the soil carefully as the pit becomes deeper and deeper since variations in soil composition can be used to identify climatic and other living conditions". "Gauge" and "monitor" are similar in meaning.

34) The correct answer is "biased". Research indicates that the interpretation of archaeological artefacts discovered in the early nineteenth century may have been *biased*. Paragraph 8 states that "recent research suggests that inherent social and cultural *biases* pervaded the

manner in which archaeological findings were investigated and explicated during the early nineteenth century". The noun "biases" from the passage needs to be changed to the adjective "biased" in order to make your answer grammatically correct.

35 and 36) The correct answers are: "consideration" and "analysis". *Consideration* was not given to the effect of affluence and nationality on the *analysis* of the artefacts. Paragraph 8 continues as follows: "little attention was paid to the roles that wealth, status and nationality played in the interpretation of the artefacts". The phrase "consideration was not given" from the answer and the phrase "little attention was paid to" from the passage are synonyms. The word "analysis" from the answer and the word "interpretation" from the passage are also synonyms.

37) The correct answer is "evolutionary". *Evolutionary* theory was established by Charles Darwin. Paragraph 9 explains that "Darwinian theory [is] the notion that human beings are the ultimate product of a long biological *evolutionary* process".

38) The correct answer is "impact". Evolutionary theory began to have an *impact* on the examination of the artefacts. Paragraph 9 also explains that evolutionary theory "infiltrated the discipline of archaeology and heavily influenced the manner in which archaeological artefacts were recovered

and analysed". The phrase "have an impact on" from the answer and the phrase "heavily influenced the manner" from the passage are synonyms.

39) The correct answer is "prejudice". The problems caused by cultural *prejudice* started to be overcome. Paragraph 9 points out that "by the middle of the 1900s, the imbalance created by the cultural biases began to be rectified". The word "prejudice" from the answer and the word "biases" from the passage are synonyms.

40) The correct answer is "amount". An increasing *amount* of artefacts were recovered from Africa and Asia at that time. The past paragraph of the passage states that "there was a *surge* in artefacts excavated from African and Asian localities". The phrase "increasing" from the answer and the word "surge" from the passage are similar in meaning.

IELTS Practice Reading – Test 3
Answer Sheet

1.   21.
2.   22.
3.   23.
4.   24.
5.   25.
6.   26.
7.   27.
8.   28.
9.   29.
10.   30.
11.   31.
12.   32.
13.   33.
14.   34.
15.   35.
16.   36.
17.   37.
18.   38.
19.   39.
20.   40.

IELTS Practice Reading – Test 3

READING PASSAGE 1

*You should spend about 20 minutes on **Questions 1 to 12** which are based on Reading Passage 1 below:*

In the Black Hills in the state of South Dakota in the United States, four visages protrude from the side of a mountain. The faces are those of four United States' presidents: George Washington, Thomas Jefferson, Theodore Roosevelt and Abraham Lincoln. Overseen and directed by the Danish-American sculptor John Gutzon Borglum, the work on this giant display of outdoor art was a Herculean task that took 14 years to complete.

A South Dakota state historian named Doane Robinson originally conceived of the idea for the memorial sculpture. He proposed that the work be dedicated to popular figures, who were prominent in the western United States and accordingly suggested statues of western heroes such as Buffalo Bill Cody and Kit Carson. Deeming a project dedicated to popular heroes frivolous, Borglum rejected Robinson's proposal. It was Borglum's firm conviction that the mountain carving be used to memorialise individuals of national, rather than regional, importance.

Mount Rushmore therefore became a national memorial, dedicated to the four presidents who were considered most pivotal in United States history. Washington was chosen on the basis of being the first president. Jefferson, who was of course a president, was also instrumental in the writing of the American Declaration of Independence. Lincoln was selected on the basis of the mettle he demonstrated during the American Civil War, Roosevelt for his development of Square Deal policy, as well as for being a proponent of the construction of the Panama Canal. Commencing with Washington's head first, Borglum quickly realised that it would be best to work on only one head at a time, in order to make it compatible with its surroundings. In order to help him visualise the final outcome, he fashioned a 1.5 metre high plaster model on a scale of 1 to 12.

Work on the venture began in 1927 and was completed in 1941. The cost of the project was nearly $1,000,000, which would be equivalent to over $70 million dollars today. The financing was raised mostly from national government funds, but also from charitable donations from magnanimous and benevolent members of the public. The carving of the mountain was tedious and exacting work, employing 360 men who worked in groups of 30. The daily working conditions on the mountainside can best be described as treacherous. For instance, men were often strapped inside leather harnesses that dangled over the cliff edge. Further, workers needed great strength to withstand the exertion of drilling into the mountainside.

The workmen faced frequent delays due to a dearth of financial backing in the early days, in addition to inclement weather throughout the 14 year period. Adverse conditions were also discovered when the carving of Jefferson began. The detection of poor quality stone on the mountain to the left of Washington resulted in Jefferson's face being repositioned to the right side. In spite of these setbacks, Mount Rushmore remained the best choice for the venue of the memorial. Yet, a large amount of the rock had to be blasted away from the mountain using dynamite or pneumatic drills, and as a result, approximately 450,000 tons of rock still lies at the foot of the mountain today.

Each of the four heads on the mountaintop is approximately 18 metres in height. Each nose is roughly 6 metres in length, while each mouth is approximately 5 metres wide. Needless to say, creating facial expressions on such an immense scale was not child's play. It required the work of a true craftsman like Borglum to give each visage its own unique character. In particular, Borglum's attention to detail on the eyes of each president was a stroke of genius. He gave the eyes a life-like quality by making each pupil hollow in order to reflect the natural sunlight.

Sadly, Borglum passed away in March of 1941, just months prior to the completion of the presidential memorial. In loving memory of his father, Lincoln Borglum, the son of John Gutzon Borglum, carried the project to completion. Having laboured on the mountain as an adolescent, Lincoln was aptly-qualified to supervise the finishing touches on this mammoth monument.

Questions 1 to 12

Choose the correct letter A, B, C or D.

1) Why did Doane Robinson suggest that the western heroes be the subject of the monument?
    A. Western heroes were well-known and loved by the public.
    B. The westward expansion movement would not have been successful without Buffalo Bill Cody and Kit Carson.

C. Such figures were of national import.

D. The dedication of a sculpture to Western heroes would raise their profiles.

2) Which of the following statements about the selection of presidents for Mount Rushmore is TRUE?

A. There was some debate about which presidents to choose.

B. These four presidents were well known internationally.

C. These presidents changed the course of United States policy and history.

D. These presidents were of some importance regionally.

3) Why was it necessary to change the location of the carving for Jefferson?

A. because of poor weather

B. due to a lack of money

C. because the rock on the original location was of inferior condition

D. since Borglum changed his mind

4) The author provides the specific measurements of the features of Mount Rushmore in order to

A. reveal that the carving lacks a sense of artistic proportion

B. underscore the imposing and impressive size of the monument

C. emphasise the importance of continuous financing for the work

D. criticise the amount of money spent on the sculpture

5) What can be inferred about the work of Lincoln Borglum?
   A. It meant that the project was completed on time.
   B. The project was behind schedule when his father died.
   C. He worked begrudgingly on the project as a teenager.
   D. He completed the monument happily and competently as a tribute to his father.

6) Which of the following statements accurately expresses the author's attitude about John Gutzon Borglum and his work?
   A. He was a talented and perceptive artist.
   B. He was profligate in his spending for the Mount Rushmore project.
   C. His work was misunderstood during his lifetime.
   D. He was an incompetent mentor for his son.

7) According to the passage, all of the following statements about Mount Rushmore are true EXCEPT
   A. The project was predominantly funded on a national level.
   B. Generous private individuals contributed financial backing for the work.
   C. Funding was plentiful at the beginning of the project.
   D. Adverse weather conditions sometimes hampered work on the project.

8-10) Select the **THREE** sentences below that express the main ideas of the passage:

A. Mount Rushmore was dedicated to presidents of crucial importance.
B. The Mount Rushmore project was beset with various difficulties.
C. Members of the public donated money towards the project.
D. The project was a large-scale, time-consuming and dangerous task.
E. The eyes of each face on the memorial are vivid and lifelike.
F. Lincoln Borglum completed the Mount Rushmore project.

11-12) Which **TWO** of the following helped John Gutzon Borglum achieve an artistic, yet realistic-looking result?

A. receiving sufficient funding
B. building a scale model
C. paying attention to detail
D. devoting the memorial to national figures

READING PASSAGE 2

*You should spend about 20 minutes on **Questions 13 to 26** which are based on Reading Passage 2 below:*

Sickly Youth

Every morning, tens of thousands of children in England under age 10 have nothing to eat or drink before leaving home for school. Research also shows that out of all youths in the 13-year-old age group, 7% are regular smokers. In addition, the consumption of alcoholic beverages among 11-15 year olds has more than doubled in the past decade, with 25% of this age group drinking on average the equivalent of over four pints of beer every week.

In spite of an overall trend for improvements in child health, inequalities in health have also been on the rise. These inequalities reveal that rates of disease and death are far higher in poorer households. Therefore, one key reason for tackling child poverty is to rectify these inequalities in child health, which carry over into adulthood. Accordingly, the government has made the commitment to attempt to lower child poverty dramatically in the next two decades.

But will this governmental commitment actually reduce child poverty and improve child health? Some say that the government's monetary support for households will invariably be spent on sweets and crisps, or other junk food, or worse, on more tobacco, alcohol and even drugs. However, providing households with more money in the form of governmental assistance gives them the opportunity to spend more on nutritious, often more expensive, food. Yet, if the government truly wishes to improve the health of poor children, it should realise that families cannot rely on only modest increases in income.

For the children leaving home without any breakfast, these government measures are not enough. A better option would be to feed the children through school breakfast and dinner programmes. Giving free school meals to children from working families would be the best and most direct way of improving child nutrition. Moreover, research from the United States demonstrates that children's learning suffers when they do not have a nutritious breakfast. In response to this research, the US government has developed programmes for nutritious school breakfasts and dinners, and more funds are now spent on this meal programme than on welfare benefits. Over seven million children receive free or reduced-price breakfasts in a programme administered by the United States Department of Agriculture.

In Great Britain, breakfast clubs have been started and now include more than 10,000 children. Nevertheless, there remains a clear need for the authorities to address nutrition as one of the worst symptoms of child poverty since children in many areas still do not get a proper breakfast and the effectiveness of their education is jeopardised as a result.

Smoking also greatly damages the health of children and increases childhood mortality rates. While the government has raised the cigarette tax, thereby increasing the cost of tobacco to consumers, this will not bring about the desired result. On the contrary, it will leave poor parents worse off, and their children will suffer. Children's health would be better served if the government re-allocated half of the resources spent on attempting to halt cigarette smuggling to preventing cigarette sales to children.

One reason for the rise in children's drinking is the increase in the consumption of 'alcopops' – fizzy, sweetened alcohol. These beverages make alcohol more attractive to young people and children. In spite of this, the government will not speak out against big business like the beverage manufacturing companies.

Improving children's opportunities depends on ending child poverty and improving the health of the poorest children. While these two aims are related, it would be foolish to believe that the reduction of child poverty would automatically improve children's nutrition and reduce their smoking and drinking. Re-thinking the governmental nutritional provision and much more effective education and prevention are still needed in order to improve child health.

Questions 13 to 17

Do the following statements agree with the information in Reading Passage 2? Write the following:

TRUE   *if the statement agrees with the information in the passage*

FALSE   *if the statement contradicts the information in the passage*

NOT GIVEN   *if there is no information in the passage on this point*

13) Children from poor families are more likely to suffer ill health.

14) Some people express scepticism about the government's plans to reduce child poverty.

15) Small increases in household income can dramatically affect children's health.

16) More than 7 million children in the United Kingdom currently receive free breakfasts.

17) The public has criticised the establishment of breakfast clubs.

Please go to the next page.

Questions 18-26

A summary of the passage is given below. Complete the summary using your own words.

*Use **ONLY ONE WORD** for each gap.*

Even though there has been an **18)** .... in child health, health inequalities have risen. The government hopes to bring about a **19)** .... in child poverty. However, **20)** .... increases in household income will be necessary in order to make a substantial improvement. The **21)** .... requirements of children must also be considered. The **22)** .... of free school dinners to working families could be one solution. Public awareness and education are also **23)** .... in order to optimise child health. The smoking tax has been **24)** ...., and children's drinking has **25)** .... Thus, there is a definite **26)** .... between child poverty and poor child health.

READING PASSAGE 3

*You should spend about 20 minutes on **Questions 27 to 40** which are based on Reading Passage 3 below:*

SECTION A:

Results of a survey on social trends have identified a rise in immigration as the most significant social change in recent years. Population patterns have changed dramatically because immigration has become the main catalyst for population growth. Homegrown population increases, defined as the surplus of births over deaths, have been surpassed by immigration. In other words, immigration has increased, while natural population growth has fallen. Specifically, at the end of the twentieth century, net inward migration increased to 194,000, while natural population growth fell to 72,000. This amounts to a shift in the significance of immigration to changes in the population, with consequences for ethnic mix and structure. Moreover, immigration patterns will also affect where people choose to live

SECTION B:

In spite of this steady influx, most people regard immigration as a very good thing which has benefited the country. Benefits include skills brought by workers needed to expand the information technology industry. The younger age profile of immigrants also helps to balance the pressures of an ageing population.

SECTION C:

The survey also revealed other important social trends relating to immigration. Notably, the population increased more than fifty percent during the twentieth century, but the number of households tripled to almost 24 million at the beginning of the twenty-first century. Nearly one-third of all households are now single-person households, which is more than two and a half times that proportion in 1961. There were 179,000 first marriages in 1999, which was less than half of the amount in 1970. The average age of women at first childbirth also increased during the same period from 26.2 to 29 years of age.

SECTION D:

The survey found that the distribution of income became more unequal at the end of the twentieth century. In 1997 the income of the richest 10% of the people in the country rose by 4% to £559.70 a week, while for the poorest it increased only 1.8% to 136.10.

The amount of consumer credit increased 115 billion in 1999, which was nearly double that of ten years earlier. Cash-only transactions fell during the last decade of the twentieth century, but still accounted for two-thirds of all transactions.

SECTION E:

The survey was carried out on the 200th anniversary of the first-ever census. In 1801 the UK population was approximately 10 million people, comprising approximately 2 million households. Since then, the population has increased six-fold, and the number of households twelve-fold. In 1821, half of the population was under the age of 20, but this proportion was only 25% in 1999.

Questions 27-31

Reading passage 1 has 5 sections A to E.

Choose the best heading for each section from the list of headings below.

List of Headings

i. Advantages of immigration

ii. Bi-centennial comparisons

iii. Credit card payments and debts

iv. Financial trends

v. Immigration and the information technology industry

vi. Immigration and population patterns

vii. Other major social trends

viii. Population change

ix. Reasons for the survey

x. Statistics on marriage and childbirth

27) Section A _____

28) Section B _____

29) Section C _____

30) Section D _____

31) Section E _____

Questions 32-37

Answer the questions below using **NO MORE THAN THREE WORDS OR NUMBERS** for each answer.

32) What term is used to describe the birth rate minus the mortality rate?

   ....

33) What was the main influence on population change at the end of the 20th century?

   ....

34) What change occurred in net migration at the end of the 20th century?

   ....

35) What was the number of households at the turn of the new millennium?

   ....

36) During the 1990s, how did most people pay for transactions?

   ....

37) Since 1801, how much has the population risen?

....

Questions 38-40

Choose **THREE LETTERS** A, B, C, D or E.

38-40) Based solely on information contained in the passage, immigration changes will affect which of the following aspects of the population?

   A. Age profile

   B. Choice of residence

   C. Income and finance

   D. Marriage rates

   E. Maternal age

   F. Population ethnicity

READING TEST 3 – ANSWER KEY

1) A

2) C

3) C

4) B

5) D

6) A

7) C

8-10) A, B, D

11-12) B, C

13) T

14) T

15) F

16) F

17) NG

18) improvement

19) reduction

20) large / larger

21) nutrition / nutritional

22) provision

23) necessary / needed / required

24) ineffective

25) increased / risen

26) relationship

27) vi

28) i

29) vii

30) iv

31) ii

32) homegrown population increase

33) immigration

34) increased to 194,000

35) 24 million

36) cash

37) six times / six-fold

38-40) A, B, F

READING TEST 3 – EXPLANATIONS TO THE ANSWERS

1) The correct answer is A. Doane Robinson suggested that the western heroes be the subject of the monument because they were well-known and loved by the public. Paragraph 2 states: "A South Dakota state historian named Doane Robinson originally conceived of the idea for the memorial sculpture. He proposed that the work be dedicated to *popular* figures, who were *prominent* in the western United States and accordingly suggested statues of western heroes such as Buffalo Bill Cody and Kit Carson". "Popular" and "prominent" are synonymous with "loved" and "well-known".

2) The correct answer is C. It is true that the presidents selected for Mount Rushmore changed the course of United States policy and history. Paragraph 3 begins as follows: "Mount Rushmore therefore became a national memorial, dedicated to the four presidents who were considered most pivotal in United States history". "Pivotal" means of central importance in bringing about change.

3) The correct answer is C. It was necessary to change the location of the carving for Jefferson because the rock on the original location was of inferior condition. Paragraph 5 states: "The detection of poor quality stone on the mountain to the left of Washington resulted in Jefferson's

face being repositioned to the right side". The phrases "rock of inferior condition" and "poor quality stone" are synonymous.

4) The correct answer is B. The author provides the specific measurements of the features of Mount Rushmore in order to underscore the imposing and impressive size of the monument. Paragraph 6 states: "Each nose is roughly 6 metres in length, while each mouth is approximately 5 metres wide. Needless to say, creating facial expressions on such an immense scale was not child's play". When the author says that the project "was not child's play", she is emphasising that the size of the monument is imposing and impressive.

5) The correct answer is D. From the passage, the reader can infer that Lincoln Borglum completed the monument happily and competently as a tribute to his father. The last paragraph states: "In loving memory of his father, Lincoln Borglum, the son of John Gutzon Borglum, carried the project to completion. Having laboured on the mountain as an adolescent, Lincoln was aptly-qualified to supervise the finishing touches on this mammoth monument". The phrase "in loving memory" shows that he finished the project happily. The adjective "aptly-qualified" is synonymous with "competently".

6) The correct answer is A. The author's attitude about John Gutzon Borglum is that he was a talented and perceptive artist. Paragraph 6 states: "It required the work of a true craftsman like Borglum to give each visage its own unique character". The phrase "a true craftsman" reveals the author's admiration for the artist.

7) The correct answer is C. The statement that funding was plentiful at the beginning of the project is not mentioned in the passage. Paragraph 4 describes the sources of funding, but it does not state that funding was higher at the start of the project.

8-10) The correct answers are: A, B, D. The main ideas of the passage are: (A) Mount Rushmore was dedicated to presidents of crucial importance; (B) the Mount Rushmore project was beset with various difficulties; and (D) the project was a large-scale, time-consuming and dangerous task. Paragraphs 2 and 3 talk about the selection of presidents of national importance; paragraphs 4 and 5 describe the practical and financial difficulties; and paragraph 6 describes the immense scale of the project, and paragraph 7 talks about the completion date of the project.

11-12) The correct answers are: B, C. The following helped John Gutzon Borglum achieve an artistic, yet realistic-looking result: (B) building a scale model; and (C) paying attention to detail. Paragraph 3 states: "In order to help him visualise the final outcome, he fashioned a 1.5 metre high plaster model on a scale of 1 to 12". Paragraph 7 states: "In particular, Borglum's attention to detail on the eyes of each president was a stroke of genius. He gave the eyes a life-like quality by making each pupil hollow in order to reflect the natural sunlight".

13) The correct answer is T. It is true that children from poor families are more likely to suffer ill health. Paragraph 2 states: "These inequalities reveal that rates of disease and death are far higher in poorer households".

14) The correct answer is T. It is true that some people express scepticism about the government's plans to reduce child poverty. Paragraph 3 states: "Some say that the government's monetary support for households will invariably be spent on sweets and crisps, or other junk food, or worse, on more tobacco, alcohol and even drugs".

15) The correct answer is F. It is false that small increases in household income can dramatically affect children's health. Paragraph 3 states: "If the government truly wishes to improve the health of poor children, it should realise that families cannot rely on only modest increases in income".

16) The correct answer is F. It is false that more than 7 million children in the United Kingdom currently receive free breakfasts since those breakfast programmes are in the United States. Paragraph 4 states: "Over seven million children receive free or reduced-price breakfasts in a programme administered by the United States Department of Agriculture".

17) The correct answer is NG. The following statement is not given in the passage: The public has criticised the establishment of breakfast clubs. The passage mentions other criticisms, but it does not mention this one.

18) The correct answer is "improvement". Even though there has been an *improvement* in child health, health inequalities have risen. Paragraph 2 states: "In spite of an overall trend for improvements in child health, inequalities in health have also been on the rise".

19) The correct answer is "reduction". The government hopes to bring about a *reduction* in child poverty. Paragraph 3 states: "Accordingly, the government has made the commitment to attempt to lower child poverty dramatically in the next two decades".

20) Possible correct answers are: large / larger. However, *large* (or *larger*) increases in household income will be necessary in order to make a substantial improvement. Paragraph 3 states: "Yet, if the government truly wishes to improve the health of poor children, it should realise that

families cannot rely on only modest increases in income". "Large" and "modest" are antonyms.

21) Possible correct answers are: nutrition / nutritional. The *nutrition* (or *nutritional*) requirements of children must also be considered. Paragraph 5 states: "There remains a clear need for the authorities to address nutrition as one of the worst symptoms of child poverty".

22) The correct answer is "provision". The *provision* of free school dinners to working families could be one solution. Paragraph 4 states: Giving free school meals to children from working families would be the best and most direct way of improving child nutrition. The gerund "giving" needs to be changed to the noun "provision" in order to make the sentence grammatically correct.

23) Possible correct answers are: necessary / needed / required. Public awareness and education are also *necessary* (or *needed* or *required*) in order to optimise child health. The last paragraph states: "Re-thinking the governmental nutritional provision and much more effective education and prevention are still needed in order to improve child health".

24) The correct answer is "ineffective". The smoking tax has been *ineffective*. Paragraph 6 states: "While the government has raised the

cigarette tax, thereby increasing the cost of tobacco to consumers, this will not bring about the desired result".

25) Possible correct answers are: increased / risen. Children's drinking has *increased* (or *risen*). Paragraph 7 states: "One reason for the rise in children's drinking is the increase in the consumption of 'alcopops'".

26) The correct answer is "relationship". Thus, there is a definite *relationship* between child poverty and poor child health. This sentence sums up the main idea of the passage.

27) The correct answer is vi. "Immigration and population patterns" is the best heading for section A. Section A states: "Results of a survey on social trends have identified a rise in immigration as the most significant social change in recent years. Population patterns have changed dramatically because immigration has become the main catalyst for population growth".

28) The correct answer is i. "Advantages of immigration" is the best heading for section B. The skills brought by workers to the information technology industry and the younger age profile of immigrants are two advantages of immigration.

29) The correct answer is vii. "Other major social trends" is the best heading for section C. Section C begins as follows: "The survey also revealed other important social trends relating to immigration".

30) The correct answer is iv. "Financial trends" is the best heading for section D. This section describes income and transactions, so it is describing financial trends.

31) The correct answer is ii. "Bi-centennial comparisons" is the best heading for section E. "Bi-centennial" and "200th anniversary" are synonyms.

32) The correct answer is "homegrown population increase". The term "homegrown population increase" is used to describe the birth rate minus the mortality rate. Section A states: "Homegrown population increases [are] defined as the surplus of births over deaths".

33) The correct answer is "immigration". The main influence on population change at the end of the 20th century was immigration. Section A states: "Results of a survey on social trends have identified a rise in immigration as the most significant social change in recent years".

34) The correct answer is "increased to 194,000". Net migration had increased to 194,000 at the end of the 20th century. Section A states:

"Specifically, at the end of the twentieth century, net inward migration increased to 194,000, while natural population growth fell to 72,000".

35) The correct answer is "24 million". There were 24 million households at the turn of the new millennium. Section C states: "The number of households tripled to almost 24 million at the beginning of the twenty-first century".

36) The correct answer is "cash". During the 1990s, most people paid cash for transactions. Section D states: "Cash-only transactions fell during the last decade of the twentieth century, but still accounted for two-thirds of all transactions".

37) Possible correct answer are: six times / six-fold. The population has risen six-fold since 1801. Section E states: "In 1801 the UK population was approximately 10 million people, comprising approximately 2 million households. Since then, the population has increased six-fold".

38-40) The correct answers are: A, B, F. Immigration changes will affect: (A) Age profile; (B) Choice of residence; and (F) Population ethnicity.

(A) Section B states that immigrants have a younger age profile;

(B) Section A states that immigration patterns will also affect where people choose to live; and (F) Section A states that the population shift will have consequences for ethnic mix and structure.

www.ingramcontent.com/pod-product-compliance
Lightning Source LLC
Chambersburg PA
CBHW080035120526
44588CB00035B/2473